Mary Ruth:

Happy Birthday !!
and many more !!

Love,
Loretta

2010

Special thanks to Joe La Rosa and Joe Hample, two great cats.
And to the intrepid Geri Thoma, a real pussycat.

Published by Willow Creek Press
P.O. Box 147, Minocqua Wisconsin 54557

Library of Congress Cataloging-in-Publication Data

Hample, Stuart E.
Happy cat day : a manifesto for an official cat holiday / by Stu Hample.
p.cm.
ISBN 1-57223-681-7 (hardcover : alk. paper)
1. Cats--Humor. I. Title.
PN6231.C23H26 2004
818'.5407--dc22
2003027627

Printed in Canada

If cats are your kind of people,
this book is for you.

FOREWORD

Being a cat is cool. Apart from the fact that folks regard us merely as cuddly companions with virtually no feelings — except for catnip.

So I figured I'll deal with these misconceptions in a book.

Which puts me in a fix. Because a bunch of scairdy-cats said, "People believe we're enigmatic, so they don't bug us to perform stupid pet tricks (Pace, Dave). Your book will blow our cover.

"Besides, people don't want to hear us whine. They'll never believe we have self-doubts because they're convinced we think we're Pet Royalty. (We are.) Write about how we're superior to dogs. Don't make trouble. Stay cool."

Well, forget it!

I'm a Go-For-All-The-Marbles kind of cat. And the Big Prize is an official Cat Holiday. Three-day weekend for everybody... Except dogs.

My cattitude is: You only have 9 lives to live, live 'em big!

So here's my book.

IT'S A SOCIAL DOCUMENT.

I was just another passive domestic pet horsing around with a fuzzy fake gray mouse (to jolly the warden) pretending I was stupid enough to believe it was real. Suddenly I caught sight of myself in a mirror going through this humiliating performance, and it hit me that us cats don't really count for diddly in this dog-oriented culture.

In a flash I decided I'm not gonna play that game any more.

Because, see, laying around on the carpet all day, waiting for somebody to come home to chuck me under the chin, was not my top career choice.

If I'd *had* a choice, I'd have picked something so the world would know me for the fabulous, fantastic feline I am.

But life's a tough buck. You're supposed to shut up and play the hand you're dealt.

Which, if I did, I'd be left with a split personality.

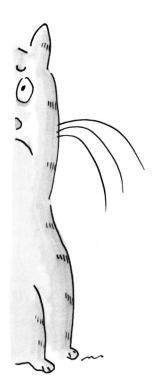

Because, on the one hand, us cats love you, our psuedo-parental owners.

11

But on the other hand, to you we're mostly just furry objects to be fed. And sometimes petted. Otherwise we're like wallpaper — in the room, but overlooked...

Which I aim to fix.

To get everybody's head straight, I'm gonna lay out some hints of what make us cats tick. Then we can get down to the crux of our mission.

Hint:

Study this cat scan

16

17

19

True, we love to be petted,
patted, caressed, cuddled,
kissed, felt, fondled, rubbed,
embraced, hugged,
nuzzled, chucked, twiddled,
massaged, dandled,
squeezed, snuggled,
and stroked
(especially behind the ears) ...

... but only when we feel like it.

TEST YOUR CAT KNOWLEDGE

TRUE or FALSE:

Cats are content
to be alone for days
with dry food and water.

Cat is a dirty word in
some quarters.
So we continually need to
prop up our egos.

Just like you do.

cat (kăt) *n.* **1.a.** A small carnivorous mammal *(Felis catus* or *F. domesticus)* domesticated since early times as a catcher of rodents and as a pet and existing in several distinctive breeds and varieties. **b.** Any of various other carnivorous mammals of the family Felidae, such as the lion. **c.** The fur of a domestic cat. **2.** A woman regarded as spiteful. **3.** A cat-o'-nine-tails.

cat·like (kăt´lik´) *adj.* Resembling a cat, esp. in being quiet or stealthy.

cat·call (kăt´kôl´) *n.* A harsh or shrill call or whistle expressing derision or disapproval. — **cat´call´** *v.*

cat·ty[1] (kat´e) *adj.* **-ti·er, -ti·est. 1.** Subtly cruel or malicious. 2. Catlike; stealthy. — **cat´ti·ly** *adv.* — **cat´ti·ness** *n.*

WEBSTER'S DICTIONARY

27

THE NEW YORK TIMES BOOK REVIEW

Best Sellers

This Week	NONFICTION	Last Week	Weeks On List
1	**HAPPY CAT DAY** by Tiger Hample. (Willow Creek Press, $14.95.) The Nobel Prize-winning billionaire feline calls for an official holiday to honor cats.	1	8,987
2	**LIES (AND THE LYING DOGS WHO BARK THEM)** by Tabby Katsman. (Simian & Shuster, $21.95.) A satirical take on the baloney of right-wing dogs.	8	7
3	**WHO'S LOOKING OUT FOR CATS?** by Kitty Calley (Litterary Press, $17.95.) Attacks those species who she feels have denigrated the cat population.	6	3
4	**DOGS FICTION: HOAX REVEALED!** By Caterina Phelan. (Whisker Books, $22.95.) Incontrovertible proof that canines don't exist, based on new historical research.	1	

US

We bathe ourselves.

THEM

US

We don't pee on living things.

THEM

US

You don't have to walk *Felis domesticus*.

THEM

US

We're the only pets who purr.

THEM

45

KITTY LITTER-ATURE

HOW MANY FAMOUS CATS CAN YOU NAME?

If you can identify more than 7, you're catapaulted into the Experts category. Being able to name no more than 2 is catastrophic. (Answers below.)

(1) Fritz the Cat, (2) The Cat In the Hat, (3) Garfield, (4) Top Cat, (5) Felix the Cat, (6) Willa Cather, (7) Krazy Kat, (8) Catfish Hunter, (9) Cat Stevens, (10) Kitty Carlisle.

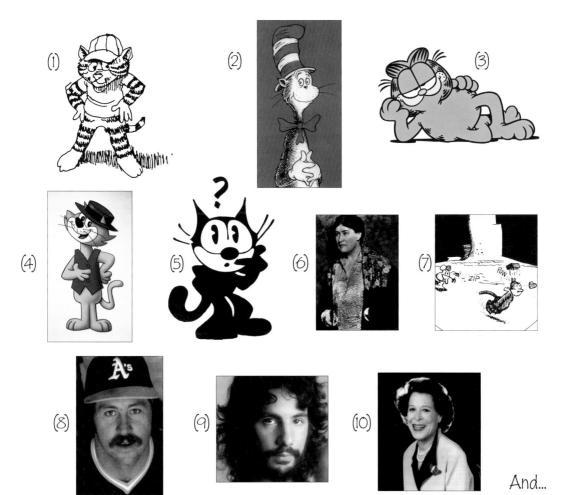

(1)

(2)

(3)

(4)

(5)

(6)

(7)

(8)

(9)

(10)

And...

49

* YOU DOUBT ME? GOOGLE "BAST" + "EGYPTIAN CAT GODDESS"

53

THE WAR ROOM

Let your voice be heard! Call your legislators (202) 224-3121 and ask for them by name. For your senators, go to www.senate.gov/ — and log on to their websites by selecting your state on the Senate web page. For your Congressional Representative, find the House website at www.house.gov. Send emails urging them all to sponsor legislation for creation of Cat Day as an official holiday — and also for issuance of a Cat Day stamp. See sample message on next page. Let them know you want action and you want it now!

[HERE'S THE KIND OF MESSAGE TO SEND]

Dear _____,

I write to bring to your attention the shocking fact that while there are a whole bunch of holidays set aside for honoring all sorts of people, causes, places, and events, there still isn't one to celebrate one of God's noblest creations — namely domestic cats (aka pussy cats, tabbys, and felines), beloved by hundreds of millions, from the lowly to the mighty. Maybe one or more are living in your home, in which case you are already familiar with the wonders of this splendid species.

Or, if you're not one of those fortunate enough to enjoy the blessings of having a cat in your life, please know that these amazing, companionable creatures, because of the many gifts they confer upon humankind, deserve to be honored with their very own national holiday.

Therefore, I urge you to employ the power of your office — along with arm-twisting and calling in chits from colleagues who owe you a big one — to bring about a resolution to establish "Cat Day," and also lobby for issuance of a Cat Day stamp, so this rank injustice will, at long last, be set right.

Sincerely yours,

(or even better, send a message in your own words.)

LONG BEFORE CAT DAY
1. Contact fellow cat lovers
2. Hit Cat Sites, chat rooms message boards
3. Hit my site HAPPYCATDAY.ORG for tips on how to:
   (a) Start a Cat Day Club.
   (b) Plan a Cat Day party
   (c) Arrange a Cat Day Parade
   (The first Parade will probably be small...)

CATS R COOL

THE FIRST ANNUAL INTERNATIONAL CAT DAY PARADE

Okay, not exactly earth-shaking ...

...but maybe someday...

PEPPY CHEERS TO REV UP FOLKS AT YOUR PARADE

Take your cat to work.

Tango with your tabby.

Spiff up the little darling.

Treat your cat to a pet-icure.

Serenade your sweetie-puss.

Snap lots of photos of you-know-who.

Honor your feline.

Give your cat the whole bed.

ON CAT DAY NIGHT

76

LET IT ALL HANG OUT!

Dream the Impossible Dream.

CAT DAY COUNCIL (CDC) OF AMERICA

This is to certify that

Ms/Mr _____

BEING A CAT PERSON, AND THUS A SUPERIOR HUMAN BEING, DEDICATES HIM/HERSELF
TO ESTABLISHMENT OF AN OFFICIAL HOLIDAY HONORING FELINES, TO BE CALLED

CAT DAY

*In witness whereof, I, Tiger Hample,
by the Authority vested in me by my
Noble Cat Lineage, hereby set my paw.*

CAT DAY FOUNDER

Download this certificate from happycatday.org, insert your name, and frame.